OCEAN DETECTIVES

Solving the Mysteries of the Sea

Mary Cerullo

RSVP

**RAINTREE
STECK-VAUGHN**

P U B L I S H E R S

A Steck-Vaughn Company

Austin, Texas

www.steck-vaughn.com

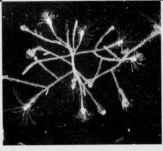

For Jeff Rotman, my partner
in underwater endeavors

Steck-Vaughn Company

First published 2000 by Raintree Steck-Vaughn Publishers,
an imprint of Steck-Vaughn Company.

Copyright © 2000 Turnstone Publishing Group, Inc.
Copyright © 2000, text, by Mary Cerullo.

Library of Congress Cataloging-in-Publication Data

Cerullo, Mary M.
 Ocean detectives: solving the mysteries of the sea / Mary Cerullo.
  p. cm. — (Turnstone ocean explorer book)
 Includes bibliographic references and index.
 Summary: Examines the scientific investigation of various problems in marine ecology,
 including the destruction of coral reefs and the endangering of penguins and salmon.
  ISBN 0-7398-1236-X (hardcover) — ISBN 0-7398-1237-8 (softcover)
  1. Marine ecology—Research Juvenile Literature. [1. Marine ecology. 2. Ecology.] I. Title.
II. Series: Turnstone ocean explorer book.
QH541.5S3C435 1999
577.7—dc21   99-20406
                        CIP

For information about this and other Turnstone reference books and educational materials,
visit Turnstone Publishing Group on the World Wide Web at http://www.turnstonepub.com.

Photo credits listed on page 64 constitute part of this copyright page.

Printed and bound in the United States of America

1 2 3 4 5 6 7 8 9 0 LB 04 03 02 01 00 99

CONTENTS

Scientific Inquiry

Make an Observation

Very few fish babies are growing to adulthood.

Ask a Question—Form a Hypothesis

Could fewer fishes be surviving because of changes in the environment?

Collect Data or Design an Experiment

a. Sample baby fishes to find out how many there are and how they find food.

b. Count the animals baby fishes eat.

c. Use computers to help count baby fishes and the animals they eat.

Draw a Conclusion

Baby fishes need just the right temperature, hiding spots, and food in order to grow. If something such as the temperature changes, that could cause the baby fishes to die.

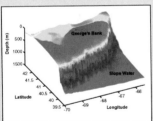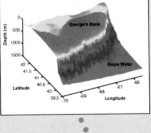

Interpret Data

Enter what you found out about baby fishes, their favorite temperatures, food, and hiding spots into a computer to make a model.

1

SCIENTISTS ARE OCEAN INVESTIGATORS

"While a detective may be trying to figure out 'Whodunit?' we want to find out what makes an animal tick—or not tick, as the case may be—as well as it should."—Biologist Carl Schreck

"Chance has put in our way a most singular and whimsical problem, and its solution is its own reward," stated Sherlock Holmes, the world's greatest fictional detective. Holmes used his amazing skills of deduction to solve mysteries in nineteenth-century London.

Generations of ocean scientists have studied undersea mysteries that would have puzzled the great detective himself. And like Holmes, scientists are intrigued as much by the problem as by the solution. Biologist Carl Schreck compares the way he studies problems to a police investigation. "Scientists do a lot of legwork, lots of homework to solve a mystery. Like detectives, we piece together clues to come up with theories about how something may have happened. Then we follow the clues, do experiments, and make observations to see which one of the theories, if any, fits the circumstances of the 'crime.'"

Whatever and wherever they are studying, all scientists employ a similar approach to their investigations—scientific inquiry. To begin, you make an observation. Next, you ask a question or make a guess based on what you observed. Scientists call this educated guess or question a hypothesis. Then, you gather and record data,

Scientists are people who always ask "Why?" One way scientists such as Carl Schreck answer this question is to conduct scientific inquiries.

5

Like detectives, scientists' tools include magnifying lenses and chemical testing kits. Sometimes scientists have to build one-of-a-kind tools to help them in their investigations, such as this water sampler being built by an ocean engineer.

analyze the clues you've collected, and draw a conclusion. It's not an entirely neat, step-by-step process because at any point you may need to go back or try a new path. And more questions can come up at any time along the way.

You may have used scientific inquiry yourself. Suppose that you notice leaves turning colors in the fall. That's an observation. Next, you ask a question or make a guess about the leaves. You guess that the reason the leaves change is that they become cold. You then experiment to find out whether your hypothesis is correct by freezing a green leaf to see if it changes color. If it doesn't, you'll need to go back and make a different hypothesis about the leaves. Scientists, too, often have to try again if the evidence they uncover doesn't match their hypothesis.

Ocean scientists use scientific inquiry to investigate mysteries all over the world, from tropical coral reefs to the icy Antarctic. One group of biological oceanographers studies the ecology of the oceans—the interactions among organisms, their surroundings, and anything affecting that environment, including humans.

These scientists study an ecosystem, a group of organisms together with their environment, by taking samples, making observations, and doing experiments. Often they use this information to create a computer model. Computer models help scientists understand how an ecosystem works. They also help scientists make predictions, such as how an ecosystem would change if water temperature rose or a species of fish disappeared.

It would be impossible for scientists to track what's happening to every creature in every part of the sea. Instead, they look at what they call indicator species, animals and plants that are typical of an area. What happens to the indicator species probably reflects what is happening to most other creatures around them.

Science at Sea

In school, mathematics, biology, chemistry, and physics are usually taught as separate subjects. But oceanographers need a working knowledge of all these subjects. Scott Gallager, a scientist at the Woods Hole Oceanographic Institution, says, "You can't be trained as an oceanographer without taking courses in physics, chemistry, advanced math, and biology. Oceanography is the sum of all these fields."

Oceanographers often need other people's help to do their work. They may work with an engineer to design a new net or with a computer programmer to create a computer model to predict where creatures will go. These scientists and engineers are about to test an oceanographic tool they built together.

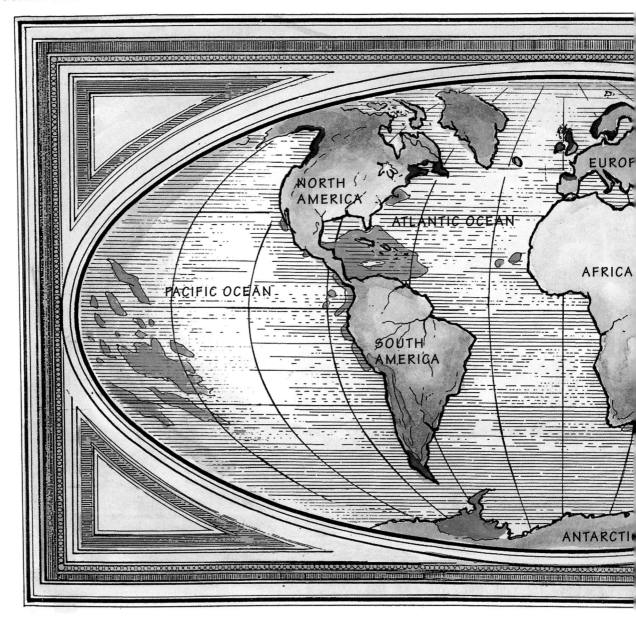

● Georges Bank
● Salmon Habitats
● Coral Reefs
● Adélie Penguins

The animals we'll examine—baby cod and haddock in the North Atlantic, tropical corals, Antarctic penguins and krill, and salmon in the Pacific Northwest—provide clues to what's happening to their worlds. By studying indicator species, ocean researchers are finding clues that human activities are changing the patterns of ocean life, patterns we are just beginning to understand.

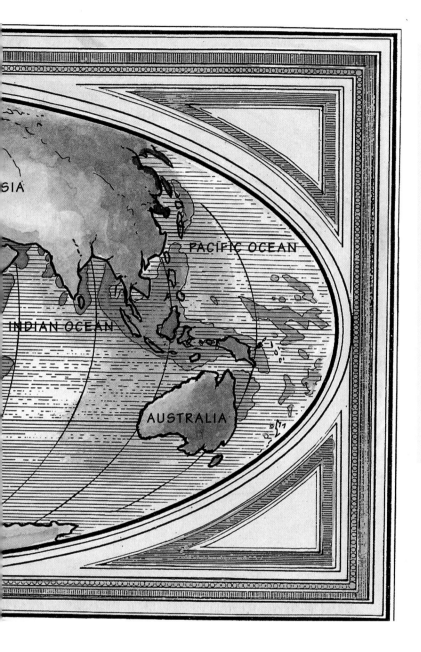

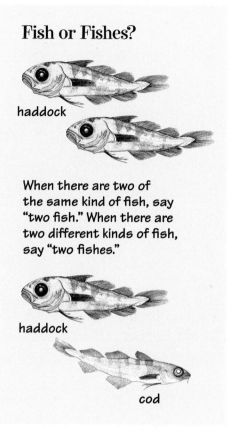

Fish or Fishes?

haddock

When there are two of
the same kind of fish, say
"two fish." When there are
two different kinds of fish,
say "two fishes."

haddock

cod

The investigations of ocean detectives are even more
important than Sherlock Holmes's capture of a thief or
the solution to a mystery. Their work is showing what
needs to be done to keep ocean life thriving and healthy.
In time, their work could be not just the early warning of
trouble in our waters, but the knowledge needed to protect life in the world's oceans.

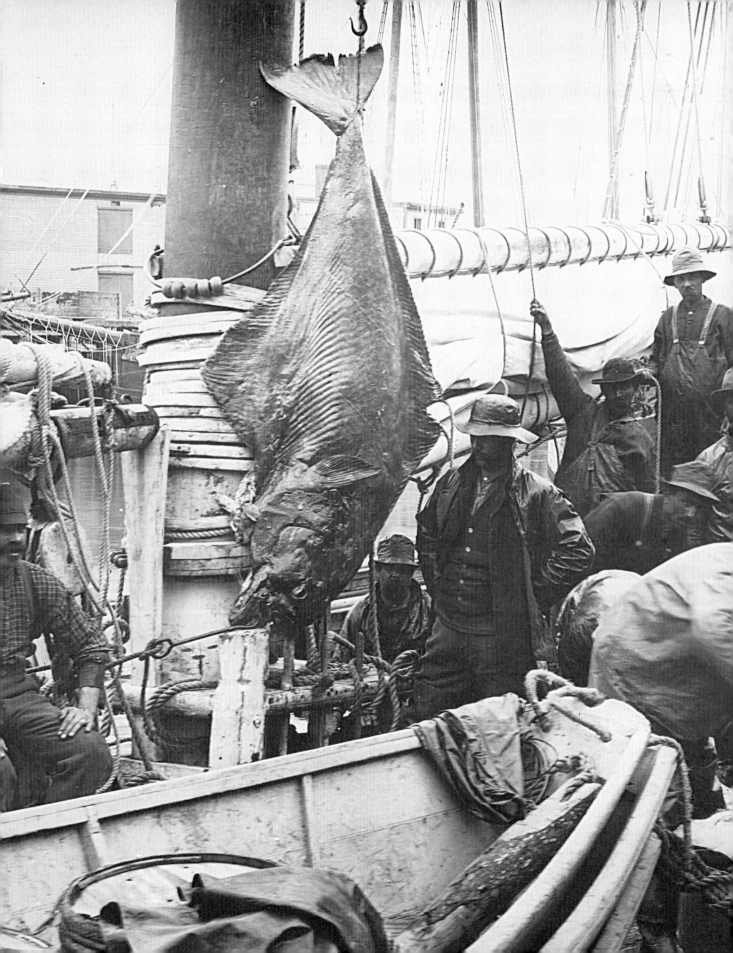

2

MYSTERY OF THE VANISHING FISHES

Georges Bank, Northwest Atlantic

Georges Bank was once one of the richest fishing areas in the world. But now overfishing has caused the huge schools of fishes to vanish. Scientists studying the fishes have found that usually 99 percent of baby fishes don't make it to their first birthday. What things kill the baby fishes of Georges Bank?

In 1497, English explorer John Cabot was mapping the North Atlantic coast of the New World and came upon Georges Bank, a shallow undersea shelf of land extending almost 321 kilometers (about 200 miles) into the Atlantic Ocean. There, he was amazed to see that "the sea is covered with fishes." In the 1500s and 1600s, many other Europeans came to harvest cod. In the 1620s, the Plymouth Pilgrims set up a profitable fishing industry on the coast of Massachusetts that quickly attracted other settlers seeking "to serve their God and to fish." Over the next century, many colonists came to pursue religious freedom and the sea's riches.

For hundreds of years, fishers worked their nets, scooping up huge quantities of the fishes of Georges Bank—cod, haddock, and yellowtail flounder—with

(above)
A wooden carving of the Sacred Cod hangs in the State House of Massachusetts as a tribute to the colonists' fishing success. Those who made their fortunes from fishing became known as the "Codfish Aristocracy."

(left)
In addition to halibut like this huge catch, 100 other species of fishes, as well as 32 species of whales, dolphins, and marine birds, were once abundant on Georges Bank.

11

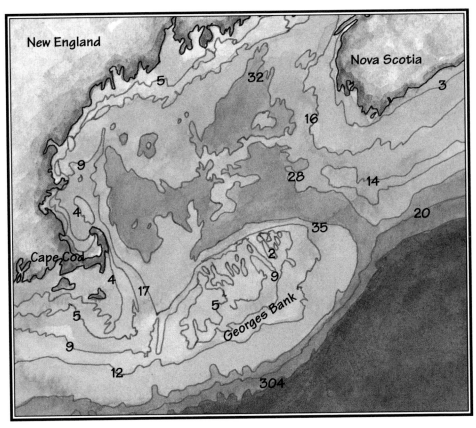

Georges Bank is part of the North American continental shelf, a shallow rim of submerged land that runs around the edge of the continent. The chart above shows the depth of the seafloor in the Gulf of Maine. The darkest blue represents the ocean seafloor. The other shades are part of the continental shelf, and the numbers show the average depth in meters. Parts of Georges Bank are so high that sunlight can reach all the way to the bank's floor. Most food production in the ocean depends on sunlight. Phytoplankton, small ocean plants that rely on sunlight to live and grow, are abundant here. They are important food for copepods, which in turn are important food for young fishes.

each pass. But the heavy nets scoured the ocean floor where fishes spawn, or lay eggs, and so destroyed many of the eggs of the next generation of fishes. Some of the fishes the nets caught were too small to keep. Even though they were thrown back, the young fishes were usually already dead, killed by the crushing weight of the other fishes in the net. Yet the sea continued to yield rich harvests of cod for hundreds of years.

By the 1970s, sophisticated new sonars—"fish finders"—showed exactly where the fishes were. Using the new techniques along with larger boats, record numbers of fishes were caught. But soon the size of the catches fell to record low levels as people took all the fishes they could find.

Despite regulations, the cod, flounder, and haddock of Georges Bank all but disappeared. In December 1994 the National Marine Fisheries Service closed about a third of Georges Bank to fishing.

This could be the end of the story of overfishing on Georges Bank. But it is just the beginning of a mystery that a team of seventy investigators is working to solve. Overfishing is the main reason for the disappearance of adult fishes on the bank, but most of the cod and haddock on Georges Bank die long before they grow large enough to be caught in a fishing net. In most years, more than 99 percent of all fishes die before they are six months old. Scientists want to know under what conditions baby fishes of Georges Bank survive or die. If they die, scientists want to know why. By determining the natural forces that kill baby fishes, scientists can make a model to determine how changes in the environment will affect fish survival. Then, they can adjust human fishing activity accordingly.

On the other hand, every year a number of young cod and haddock manage to live long enough to reach adulthood. If scientists could find out what helps these fishes survive, it could be the key to making the fishes abundant on the bank again.

Peter Wiebe, an ocean scientist at Woods Hole Oceanographic Institution (or WHOI, pronounced "HOO-ee") in Woods Hole, Massachusetts, is the project leader for the Georges Bank GLOBEC (Global Ocean Ecosystems Dynamics) program. GLOBEC was formed to study how climate change might affect life in the world's oceans. On Georges Bank changing temperatures in the water may be part of the reason baby fishes don't survive.

The GLOBEC Mystery: How Is Global Warming Affecting Life in the Sea?

The goal of GLOBEC is to predict the future of ocean animals in the face of global climate change. The Georges Bank project is the first of several GLOBEC ocean studies that will take place around the world. These projects will examine how changes in the world's climate may affect life in the ocean.

As air warms, so does water. Scientists are noticing changes in the ocean food chains in places as far apart as Antarctica and coral reefs off Florida. The changes may be due to global warming.

Satellites can provide information for scientists on what's happening globally. Images like the one above of Georges Bank show the patterns of heat released from the earth and the ocean. Images taken over time can help scientists track changes in the climate. In this image the warmest water appears red. Cooler waters appear in this order from cool to cold: yellow, green, blue.

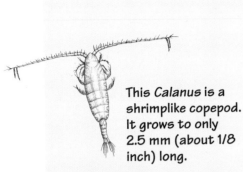

This *Calanus* is a shrimplike copepod. It grows to only 2.5 mm (about 1/8 inch) long.

⊢ actual length

Copepods are tiny cousins of lobsters and crabs. They are the most abundant animals in the ocean, possibly the most abundant on Earth, with an estimated population of one quintillion (the number 1,000 followed by 15 zeroes). If people shared all the copepods in the world equally, everyone could have one billion copepods.

What would we do with them all? We could feed most of the ocean's animals. Copepods are such an important food for baby fishes, crabs, and the other animals we eat that their number affects the amount of food humans can take from the sea. If there aren't enough copepods, there won't be enough seafood for us to eat.

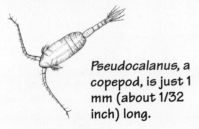

Pseudocalanus, a copepod, is just 1 mm (about 1/32 inch) long.

⊢ actual length

To find out, a multiyear project is under way to study the climate, water movement, and zooplankton, small swimming animals that are important food for young fishes on Georges Bank. Peter explains, "Fundamentally, what we're trying to do is figure out how nature works by taking apart an ecosystem bolt by bolt."

Scientists involved in the Georges Bank GLOBEC project suspect that global warming, the heating of the earth's atmosphere, may affect the survival of young fish. To find out, they are gathering evidence on the things that influence the fishes' survival, such as predators, or animals that eat them. Prey, or animals they eat, and competitors for food and space are also factors. Scientists are also studying Georges Bank's plants, water, currents, atmosphere, and ocean floor. All this information will be entered into a computer to make a model of Georges Bank. The model will show how everything works together. It will also help predict how changes such as less fishing or global warming might affect how many fishes survive. This information will help others make decisions about how to protect the larval, or baby, fishes on Georges Bank.

To make the model, the GLOBEC scientists chose four indicator species to study: baby cod, baby haddock, and two types of copepods, shrimplike creatures that are food for the growing cod and haddock. All of these animals are zooplankton, and each of them starts out smaller than the *o* in *cod*.

"Zooplankton are very important," explains oceanographer Cabell Davis, "because they're near the bottom of the food chain, feeding all other animals directly or indirectly. Most animal species in the ocean are zooplankton for at least part of their lives."

GLOBEC scientists are trying to find out all they can about these zooplankton. What they find out will help them understand the food chain of the whole ecosystem.

Every month between January and July, research ships, like the one from Woods Hole, Massachusetts, set out to investigate Georges Bank. From WHOI, Peter Wiebe, GLOBEC scientists, and crew members collect tiny, floating plants called phytoplankton along with zooplankton and water samples from forty places around Georges Bank. They also record the speed and direction of water currents, water temperature, and other information to help build a picture of Georges Bank through the seasons.

In addition to collecting general data, GLOBEC scientists also investigate specific mysteries. For example, zooplankton specialist Scott Gallager wants to find out where baby fishes live at different seasons of the year. He thinks that may have something to do with their survival. Scott also wants to find out at what depth they live and how well they survive there. "For example, we know that cod and haddock spawn between January and March on the northern tip of Georges Bank, so we have a cruise to study eggs and early larvae then." Despite the worst weather of the year in an area famous for shipwrecks, Scott and the crew work around the clock collecting samples of baby cod and haddock.

From samples taken so far, they have learned that baby fishes are very sensitive to the amount of light in the water. Without enough light, the fishes can't see their prey. If there's too much light, they're blinded, like when you look at the sun. Either way, they starve. Baby fishes need just the right amount of sunlight to survive.

While Scott Gallager chases baby cod and haddock around Georges Bank, Cabell Davis pursues copepods, the first food of newborn cod and haddock. Cabell is interested in finding out

Baby cod measure about 2.5 cm (almost 1 inch) long.

├──────────┤ actual length

Under Study

GLOBEC scientists are studying different species— baby cod and baby haddock, along with two of the copepods they eat, Calanus and Pseudocalanus.

A baby haddock at 2.5 cm (almost 1 inch) long is near the bottom of the food chain, at least until it grows bigger.

├──────────┤ actual length

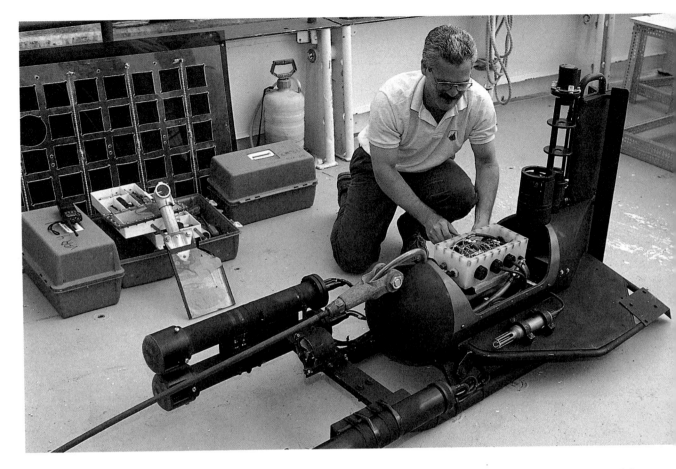

The Video Plankton Recorder, shown here with scientist Cabell Davis, is usually towed behind a ship. But it can also be mounted on a remote-controlled submersible. Like a regular microscope, the Video Plankton Recorder has both high and low settings, for seeing close up and very close up. The low setting takes pictures of an area about four to six centimeters square (about two inches square).

what affects the survival of copepods. He explains his work as taking "a series of snapshots" of where the copepods live and how many there are in each place. That will help the scientists make a computer model of copepod and fish populations on Georges Bank. "We're focusing on a few species and looking at what affects them," says Cabell.

To uncover the secrets of Georges Bank, Cabell, Scott, and WHOI engineers designed and built an underwater microscope, which they named the Video Plankton Recorder. It was designed to videotape all kinds of plankton, or tiny drifting plants and animals.

While the recorder's cameras take pictures, other instruments the recorder carries note the time, water depth, temperature, and salinity, or saltiness, of the water, and the location. So not only can Scott and Cabell see their subjects in action, they can also analyze the physical characteristics of the places where the animals are found.

At least, that's how it's supposed to work. When the ship is tossing in twenty-foot waves, it's easy for equipment to break or fall to the bottom of the ocean. When experiments go wrong or instruments fail, scientists have to be prepared to change their plans. Cabell takes it all in stride. Turning obstacles into opportunities is all part of ocean science. "It's detective work at its best. It requires you to investigate things you wouldn't even think of until you get out there."

When the system works, the Video Plankton Recorder takes sixty pictures a second. That means that at the end of a cruise, there are thousands of images to review. To help with the job, scientists created a computer program that analyzes the images, catalogs the animals by species, and selects the best pictures for scientists to examine.

Another way that scientists find out about ocean life is by using echo sounders. An echo sounder works by sending sound waves out into the water. The waves bounce back as echoes from objects, such as plankton, through the water. This can help scientists find out where different animals live around the bank. All the information collected is entered into the computer to add to the computer model.

The GLOBEC cruises have provided many new clues about where the indicator species live on Georges Bank, what times they are most plentiful, and where they go in different seasons. The scientists have learned, for example, that young copepods swim into deeper, colder waters before June when the surface waters become too warm for them. There they lie until they wake up in early winter and molt, or shed their shells, and turn into adults.

The Video Plankton Recorder's high setting covers an area about 2.5 centimeters (about 1 inch) square. One copepod or baby fish just about fills the screen.

The Video Plankton Recorder is used to study phytoplankton and zooplankton like these (top and middle) jellyfish colonies Nanomia and *Clytia*, and also *Calanus*, a copepod (bottom).

Seawater's temperature and saltiness vary from place to place and at different times of the year. The device shown above is called a CTD. This is short for Conductivity, Temperature, and Depth. It measures the conductivity (saltiness) and temperature of seawater at different depths.

Knowing where copepods live at different times of the year may help scientists predict where and when this important food supply can be found by the other creatures also living on the bank. However, Scott has discovered that even if baby cod and haddock end up in the same place as the copepods, the larval fishes may not necessarily be able to find them.

He learned that many things affect a baby fish's ability to see and find its prey. Cloudy water, weather conditions, waves, and even the angle of the sun, which changes with the seasons, can prevent hungry young fishes from finding copepods. Global warming may also play a part. Warmer temperatures may drive young fishes or their food to a cooler place, separating the baby fishes from their prey.

Too many predators can also spell disaster for larval fishes. Scientists have found many more predators feeding on baby fishes than they had expected.

The GLOBEC investigators may never be able to completely solve the mystery of why so many cod and haddock die before their first birthdays. But they hope to use the information that they are collecting to understand the best conditions for the fishes to survive. Understanding all the things that affect young fishes—from predators and prey to weather conditions and water temperature—may help scientists discover ways to help more baby fishes grow to adulthood.

The scientists' work gives information that forms the beginnings of a computer model for Georges Bank. Part

This net is one of the tools GLOBEC scientists use. It opens and closes underwater to collect samples of plants and animals at different depths.

of that model is a food web that shows how creatures in an ecosystem are connected by what they eat. The web is made of several food chains, or lines that show how energy moves as animals eat plants or other animals.

The model will allow scientists to monitor how things in Georges Bank change over time and help predict the bank's future. Cabell declares, "You can't really understand how global warming is going to affect fisheries and other marine populations until you understand how the whole system works."

Who's Eating Whom?
Georges Bank Food Web

This food web of Georges Bank shows the food relationships involving young cod and haddock. In this web, phytoplankton are at the bottom. They are eaten by microzooplankton, which are extremely small zooplankton. Copepods eat both phytoplankton and microzooplankton. Everything then branches out from the copepods. The copepods are eaten by tiny invertebrate predators and baby cod and haddock. They are prey, or food, for even some of the largest animals in the ocean, right whales and humpback whales. The baby cod and haddock are eaten by larger fish, which are then eaten by even larger animals such as dolphins and seals. Using computers, scientists ask a question such as, "What if all the baby cod disappeared?" and determine how the model would change.

Copepods

Copepods are key animals in the ocean food web. They are the main food for many larger animals, such as invertebrate predators, right and humpback whales, and baby fishes. If they disappeared, the food web might collapse.

Phytoplankton

Called "the grass of the sea," these microscopic plants are food for both copepods and other zooplankton.

eaten by

eaten by

eaten by

Microzooplankton

These are microscopic animals that feed on phytoplankton and are, in turn, eaten by copepods.

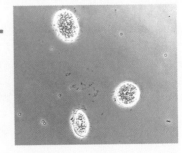

Right Whales and Humpback Whales

Whales are only at Georges Bank during the summer, so they are part of the food web for only a few months of each year.

eaten by

Herring and Mackerel

Herring and mackerel eat the smaller baby cod and haddock, and they eat more of them than investigators had expected.

eaten by

eaten by

Larval Cod and Haddock

Scientists are looking for ways to bring these fishes back to Georges Bank.

eaten by

Dolphins and Seals

Dolphins and seals come to Georges Bank for herring and mackerel. If those fishes disappeared, the dolphins and seals would probably hunt for food somewhere else.

eaten by

Invertebrate Predators

These tiny creatures feed on the even tinier copepods.

3

WHAT'S KILLING THE CORAL REEFS?

Tropical Seas

Scientists studying corals were shocked to find formerly healthy coral reefs bleached white, like skeletons. They wonder what is threatening one of the most critical ecosystems under the sea.

O n Georges Bank the water is so thick with plankton that scuba divers can barely see their own outstretched hands through the underwater fog. But tropical seas are so clear that divers can sometimes see a hundred feet or more in any direction. That's because there are few suspended sediments or phytoplankton to block their view. Compared to the cold, nutrient-filled waters of Georges Bank, tropical seas are biological deserts.

In the tropical ocean, the only concentration of large animals and shelter for miles around is at coral reefs. Though poor in dissolved nutrients and phytoplankton, coral reefs are rich in beautiful and colorful fishes, sponges, and corals. Animals fill every corner of the reef, seeking food, protection, and mates. Like an oasis in the desert, a healthy reef is critical for its residents, who have no other place to find food within easy reach.

Coral reefs are also shelter for an estimated 25 percent of all the ocean's species, including about 3,500 species of fishes and 600 species of reef-building corals. No other place on Earth, except possibly the rainforest,

(above)
Bleached corals are evidence that something is not right in tropical seas. "When you see a bleached coral reef, it literally looks as though it has snowed underwater," says researcher Tom Goreau of the Global Coral Reef Alliance.

(left)
Crowded, colorful, and bursting with activity both day and night, a healthy coral reef is like a city under the sea.

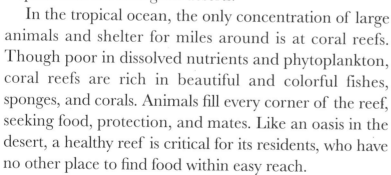

23

(above)
Coral polyps stay in their limestone "houses" during the day.

(above right)
At night coral polyps reach out their stinging tentacles to catch food. Most only come out at night, when it's less likely that predators will be hunting.

can match these underwater oases for their variety of creatures.

The rich, vibrant life of the coral reef depends on a partnership between microscopic algae, a kind of marine plant, and coral, an animal about the size of a pea.

Coral reefs are the creation of two main architects—an animal called the coral polyp and algae called zooxanthellae. Small and vase-shaped, each coral polyp takes calcium carbonate out of the water to build a limestone house, a kind of outside skeleton. This skeleton forms beneath and around a polyp's base. When a polyp dies, its skeleton remains. The next generation of coral grows on top of colonies of skeletons, forming a reef.

Coral polyps couldn't build a reef without their algal companions. Single-celled zooxanthellae live in a thin layer of polyp tissue. This tissue connects the polyp's limestone skeleton to its neighboring polyps.

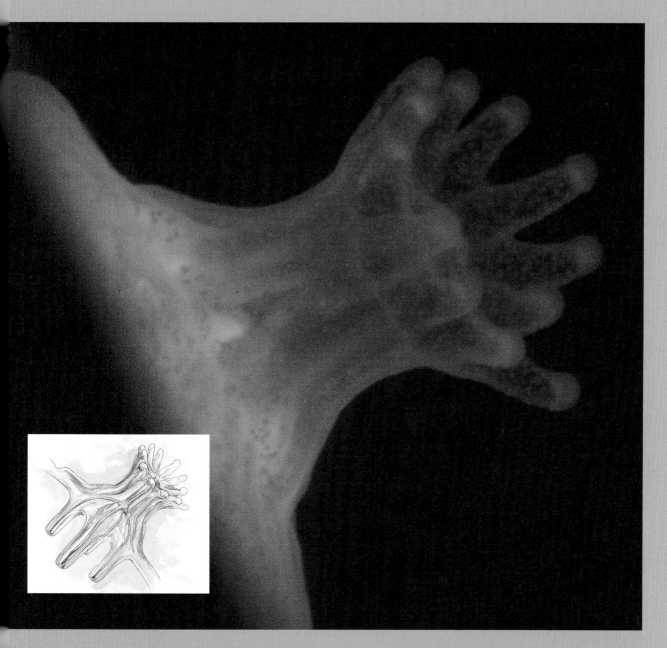

Breaking Up Is Hard to Do

The coral animal and its algae form a symbiotic relationship, which means the two different species live together. Under normal conditions, one or both species benefit from the partnership. But what happens when there's trouble? The coral, cemented for life, can't run away, so it's the algae that leave. Does the stressed coral evict its companions, or do the algae leave on their own? Scientists aren't sure. Some researchers think the zooxanthellae are more sensitive to unhealthy conditions than the corals are, and they leave before things get worse. Other scientists suspect that zooxanthellae move on because the stressed corals can no longer provide enough nutrients for the algae to grow. Why these partners split up is a mystery that scientists have yet to solve.

Coral polyps and zooxanthellae have a real partnership. Although coral polyps catch and eat tiny animals, food also comes from the zooxanthellae. Zooxanthellae use energy from the sun to make food. Coral polyps feed on nutrients that come from this process. (Scientists have found that coral polyps sometimes get more food from zooxanthellae than from catching plankton!) In turn zooxanthellae use wastes from coral polyps as nutrients.

Zooxanthellae help coral polyps remove calcium carbonate from seawater to build their limestone outer skeletons. They also give the corals their beautiful colors. Most coral polyps don't have any color of their own. The algae can make them appear pink, yellow, orange, purple, red, blue, or brown. Without the algae, you'd be able to see right through the coral's soft tissues to the white limestone underneath.

Coral reefs need warm water, but if the water gets too hot, it can be devastating for them. Divers have watched in dismay as whole reefs turned ghostly white in a matter of days. Scientists call this coral bleaching, a natural disaster in which some or all of the zooxanthellae leave. If ocean conditions return to normal, the zooxanthellae that stayed behind begin to grow again and the coral recovers. If not, the corals die.

Scientists have been discovering cases of coral bleaching for nearly a century. Some bleachings before 1982 were caused by an obvious, local culprit. Hot water from coastal power plants may pour onto a coral reef, causing bleaching. Corals in shallow water or those that live in tidepools, where they are cut off from the rest of the sea, may also bleach under the hot noon sun.

Then, beginning about 1982, scientists began to observe cases of "mass bleaching" where huge areas of

(above)
Most tourists on tropical islands are unaware that they may have parrotfish to thank for some of the sand under their feet. A parrotfish feeds on the algae that coat dead coral or on the zooxanthellae inside living coral. Its teeth have fused together to make a strong, beaklike scraper that peels off chunks of coral. These coral pieces pass through the parrotfish's digestive system, creating sand. In some places one ton of coral skeletons for each acre of coral reef is turned into sand each year, at least partly by parrotfish, nature's recyclers.

(left)
You can see where the top of this coral has bleached.

Other Coral Reef Threats

It's not only bleaching that threatens the reef. Coral reefs can also suffer from pesticides washing in from large farms and oil from offshore spills. Work at construction sites or heavy rains from a hurricane can send mudslides over fragile reefs. Sewage, fertilizers, and other nutrients

spilling onto coral reefs from nearby coasts may also allow mats of algae to grow unchecked. In the photograph at left, algae have smothered the reef. Corals weakened by human actions are less able to resist natural threats from predators, diseases such as infection from a fungus, and storms.

People working in and traveling across ocean waters can also endanger the reef. Overfishing can harm coral reefs by upsetting reef food chains. Fishers in some countries use the poison cyanide and also dynamite to catch fish. Sailors and ship captains sometimes drop anchors on reefs. All these practices can damage or destroy reefs.

coral reefs—sometimes thousands of miles across—suffered. The fact that some of these areas were far from land, people, and obvious causes was even more disturbing. Why would coral bleaching happen in these places?

That is the mystery Thomas Goreau of the Global Coral Reef Alliance has been investigating for nearly twenty years. He has visited coral reefs around the world to witness and record coral bleaching. In some places, he has found that up to 99.9 percent of the corals are affected. Tom notes, "If the stress continues or gets worse, bleaching is just the first step toward death."

Why is this happening? To find an answer, Tom matched up field observations from scientists and sports divers with data from satellites. He and fellow researchers Raymond Hayes and Al Strong mapped bleaching events and climate patterns around the world. Using all this evidence, they have reached a startling conclusion. Tom says, "Every mass bleaching follows a period of time when the temperature of the seawater increased as little as 1°C (1.8°F)

above the average temperature for the warmest month of the year. If it gets to be hotter than what corals are used to for a month or longer, the corals bleach. If it gets to be 2° to 3°C (3.6° to 5.4°F) above normal, they die."

Based on their research, Tom, Ray, and Al have predicted many bleaching events since 1990. Tom notes, "We're able to tell where it's happening, as it's happening, without even going to the field.

"The 1980s and 1990s are the hottest decades on record since temperature measurements began 150 years ago. The increase in global temperature is a worldwide phenomenon; tropics are affected as well as colder areas. But there's a very important difference between what happens in the coral reefs and what happens in the world's other ecosystems.

"If the ecosystem of Georges Bank, for example, became too hot for the animals, they would migrate

A Valuable Resource

This is a healthy reef. You can tell where the reef is by the line of waves breaking over the reef and by the change of color in the water. Reefs mark the border between deep and shallow water.

Coral reefs work as barriers, breaking incoming waves. This helps protect shorelines from erosion and beaches and waterfront homes from being damaged in large storms.

Coral reefs are also valued for medical uses. Drugs and medicines derived from reef creatures, such as sponges, sea squirts, and corals, have been used to treat cancer, AIDS, arthritis, asthma, and even broken bones.

In 1987, a group of Florida charter boat captains got together to help the reefs in their area. From this effort, Reef Relief was born. The organization helps educate divers, fishers, and boaters about how to avoid damaging reefs. Above are Reef Relief founder and Director of Marine Projects Craig Quirolo (right) with fishers from Long Bay, Jamaica.

north and be replaced by immigrants coming from the south. There would be a nearby supply of animals and plants that are adapted to the conditions. But in the warmest habitats, there is no pool of organisms to replace those that can't take it if it gets too hot. That makes coral reefs the most threatened ecosystems in the world by climate change."

Recent research has shown that high water temperature is just one factor involved in coral bleaching. Other forms of stress, including toxic pollutants and increased dissolved nutrients from sewage, may also cause bleaching. This bleaching is made worse when combined with high temperatures.

Different organizations, such as the Global Coral Reef Alliance and Reef Relief, are working to educate governments, industry, fishers, and others who use the reefs about ways to protect this resource from pollution, harmful fishing practices, and global warming. At the same time, ocean scientists are also working to find new ways to help coral reefs.

Now Tom's work focuses on coral reef recovery. He is currently involved in a project that creates artificial limestone reefs on which young corals can settle and grow. Tom's project is just one of the ideas ocean detectives are exploring as they look for ways to revive and renew our world's coral reefs.

In the Maldives in the Indian Ocean, Tom Goreau and Wolf Hilbertz are using technology to restore damaged coral reefs. Here Tom uses low-voltage electricity to take minerals out of seawater to build artificial limestone reefs.

ARE PENGUINS IN PERIL?

Antarctica

Something is upsetting the simple food chain of the Antarctic, putting young penguins in danger.

As a scientist, or even as a tourist, you couldn't find a more dramatic contrast than between a healthy tropical coral reef and the ice-encrusted waters surrounding Antarctica. While tropical reefs have a huge number of species, there are few species in the cold waters of the Atlantic Ocean, South Pacific Ocean, and South Indian Ocean that come together around the Antarctic continent. That's because not many animals can cope with water temperatures that range from -1.9°C (28°F) to 0.1°C (32.18°F). That's pretty chilly, especially when you remember that fresh water freezes at 0°C (32°F)!

Almost all the creatures of the frigid Antarctic waters feed on one thing—krill. Krill look like pink shrimp, and they are about the length of your thumb. Krill eat mostly phytoplankton, the tiniest plants in the sea.

Krill can live for seven or eight years, if they aren't eaten by penguins, sea birds, fishes, squids, seals, or some of the largest animals in the world, blue whales and humpback whales. As adults, krill may gather in such huge schools that they can turn the surface water pink.

(above)
Krill spawn, or reproduce, in the summer. Young krill spend their first winter tucked into pockets in the underside of the ice, hiding from predators and feeding on algae that coat the bottom of the ice like a fuzzy blanket.

(left)
Adélie penguins always return to the same nest site. Each nest is a pile of small rocks that holds two greenish eggs. For the next 32 days, Mom and Dad take turns sitting on the eggs. Later, parents take turns finding food for the chicks.

South Atlantic
Ocean

King George Island

Winter Ice

Summer Ice

Antarctic
Peninsula

Permanent Ice

Ross Sea

SOUTH POLE

ANTARCTICA

South Indian
Ocean

South Pacific
Ocean

As one of the last remote regions on Earth, Antarctica appeals to more adventurous investigators. Winter air temperature hovers around −51°C (−60°F). Should anything go wrong, rescue is almost impossible because the surrounding water is frozen, and a plane's systems freeze in the extreme cold. To stay for the winter here is an icy accomplishment.

Usually, though, they stay in deep water during the day to avoid predators and only rise to the surface to feed at night.

Krill are probably the most important Antarctic creatures, at least as far as the food chain is concerned. But the animal that symbolizes Antarctica to most people is an animal that feasts on krill, the penguin. Seven species of penguins visit the region. Only two, the Adélie and the Emperor penguins, breed on the Antarctic continent. Scientists who have been studying bird life here for several years are beginning to suspect that all is not well with the penguins of Antarctica.

For more than twenty years, Susan and Wayne Trivelpiece of the Southwest Fisheries Science Center in La Jolla, California, have been observing Adélie penguin breeding behavior on King George Island near the tip of the Antarctic Peninsula. Susan explains, "We have been using penguins as an indicator species to monitor the health of the Antarctic ecosystem." They started studying Adélies and their main food source, krill, in 1976 to try to learn, among other things, whether krill fishing might threaten the Antarctic food chain. Krill are harvested primarily for use in animal feed. They are also used in fertilizer. How much krill, they asked, could be

taken by people without robbing Antarctic animals of their main food supply? Since it was hard to track the tiny krill, they decided to look at krill predators instead.

From October to March, the Antarctic summer, when temperatures average about a balmy 0°C (32°F), Susan and Wayne keep track of all the Adélie penguins in their King George colony. They also attach satellite and radio tags to the parents so they can track where and how long the penguins go to feed in the sea.

Susan and Wayne Trivelpiece spend their Antarctic summers at the Copacabana Field Station (named for a famous beach in Brazil) on King George Island. In the summer, Susan says, "You can go out in shorts and a T-shirt, but you always bring along extra clothing. In five minutes the weather can go from sunny to blizzard conditions."

(above)
Here you can get a good idea of the number of penguins at Copacabana station. On the right is a blind, a place where scientists can keep warm and watch penguins without disturbing them.

(right)
Susan and Wayne help attach bands to the Adélie penguin chicks at the station. Using signals from the tags, satellites keep track of each penguin's movements, in and out of the water.

Each year Susan and Wayne put flipper bands on 1,000 Adélie chicks, too. They then count how many of these show up again two years later. Through their bird counts, Susan and Wayne found that the number of young penguins has dropped almost 50 percent in eight years. At the same time there was a dramatic drop in the krill population.

But the research team didn't find a link between the loss of these young penguins and the krill fishery. Instead, they found that both the adult penguin and krill populations rose and fell with the amount of pack ice surrounding Antarctica in the winter.

Susan explains, "Larval [baby] krill depend on the winter pack ice [floating ice that's pushed together into

one big mass of ice]. If the pack ice is heavy and extends over large areas where the krill spawn, then most of the newly hatched krill will survive. If the larval krill can't get to the ice because it's too far away, they starve." Temperature records show that fifty years ago, four out of every five Antarctic winters were cold enough to produce a big ice cover, an ideal place for larval krill to feed, hide, and grow. Now there's a "heavy ice" winter only twice every six to eight years. The research done by Susan, Wayne, and other Antarctic investigators reveals that these years match with a larger number of krill. The "boom year" krill help keep the food chain of the Antarctic going until the next "baby boom" comes along.

Krill: Masters of Survival

How do adult krill survive the long Antarctic winter with nothing to eat? No one knows for sure. Krill can live as long as two hundred days without being fed. When food is scarce, they can actually become smaller. Speaking of food, German scientists working in Antarctica around 1900 discovered that krill are edible. One wrote in his journal that "they tasted quite good, but were rather small and tiresome to peel."

Susan (on right) and a research assistant are weighing and measuring Adélie penguin chicks. The chick is put gently in the bag Susan is holding before weighing. Keeping records of the size and weight of penguin chicks helps scientists know how well the chicks are doing.

In years when cold winters produced a lot of ice, there were also a lot of krill, and most of the penguin chicks born that year returned two years later to the rookery, where penguins mate and lay eggs.

In warmer winters when there was less ice, fewer chicks survived. Researchers suspect that the young animals died at sea because of starvation or because they became too weak to escape predators. Many of the chicks they banded were never seen again.

Shrinking ice cover and rising temperatures tell scientists that the coldest place on Earth is getting warmer, and that may have serious consequences for the animals living there. In the last fifty years, winter temperatures in the peninsula region of the Antarctic have risen by 4°C to 5°C (7°F to 9°F).

This leads scientists to the next mystery: "Why is the water getting warmer?" On this, researchers don't agree. They debate whether the warming in parts of Antarctica is the result of normal climate change—the long, slow temperature changes that happen over millions of years—or early evidence of global warming.

Susan believes that in theory, krill may have evolved a long life in response to heavy ice every six to eight years during the warmer conditions in the distant past. The krill can serve as food for other animals and as a breeding stock until new "boom year" krill come along. Though until recently they no longer needed a long lifespan, they kept the adaptation.

In the late 1980s, the amount of krill that oceanographers collected in their nets dropped to about one-tenth of the normal amount. At the same time, scientists

Cold Water Survival

The animals that live in the Antarctic are well adapted to life in near-freezing water. Whales and penguins have blubber to keep them warm. Penguins also have closely packed feathers (up to seventy per square inch). They waterproof their feathers using oil from a gland near the tail.

Unlike penguins and whales, krill are cold-blooded, so they don't have to keep warm. Krill's body fluids have about the same salt level as the surrounding seawater, so they don't freeze until the water does.

Susan Trivelpiece keeps a journal as she does her fieldwork in the Antarctic. She's using pencil and paper because working in the middle of a flock of penguins is just too messy, oily, and cold a job to have a computer around.

began to see the Antarctic penguin population decreasing. "Since then, the decline has leveled off," says Susan. "The penguin population has stabilized and adjusted to the available food source and conditions. The animals are pretty resilient." Although they aren't worried that Adélie penguins are in danger of dying out, Susan and Wayne Trivelpiece continue to make their annual census so they can sound the alarm if their results point to another plunge in the penguin population.

Antarctica Is a Continent for Research

Antarctica is a "Zone of Peace" dedicated to science. The Antarctic Treaty was signed in 1959 by 12 nations. By 1994, 42 countries had signed on, representing two-thirds of the world's population. The treaty reserves the region for peaceful purposes, prohibits nuclear explosions and radioactive waste, establishes environmental protections for the region, and encourages international cooperation in scientific research.

The goal of this research is to help us understand the region and its ecosystems. Scientists in the Antarctic are also working to understand the area's effects on and responses to global processes such as climate change.

CAN WE MAKE OUR NEIGHBORHOODS SAFE FOR SALMON?

Northeast Pacific Ocean

Researchers in the northwest United States are trying to learn how salmon respond to changes humans have made in the environment. Can salmon handle the stresses these changes put on them?

A salmon travels thousands of watery miles during its brief life. As many as 1,000 miles of its journey are along the rivers of the Pacific Northwest, where the problems it encounters are created by the humans who share these waters. Along with the problems other sea creatures face, such as overfishing and global warming, the Pacific salmon must cope with environmental hazards that threaten the two things it needs most—clean, cold water and a clear route between the stream where it was born and the ocean.

High in a mountain stream, a mother salmon digs out a place in the gravel bottom with her tail. She lays thousands of eggs into the hole as a male waits nearby. After he fertilizes the eggs with a cloud of sperm, the mother covers them with more gravel. Then their life's work is complete, and the salmon seem to age overnight. Their last act as parents is to die, recycling themselves into nutrients to fertilize the waters in which their babies will grow.

(above)
This female coho salmon is spawning, or laying eggs. Afterward, she will die.

(left)
Migrating salmon are tough fish. They can run powerful rapids and jump as high as 3 1/2 meters (almost 12 feet).

How Do Salmon Find Their Way?

A salmon returns to the very stream where it was hatched years before. How does it know where to go? It's an unsolved mystery. To study the mystery, researchers act like detectives, implanting a small identification tag or radio transmitter in each fish. Like the detective's "bug," the transmitters let scientists track each salmon as it passes by a transmitter detector at a dam or on a boat.

Scientists know almost nothing about how salmon find their way across the ocean. They suspect the fish can detect the earth's magnetic field. They think salmon may also sense electric signals made when two ocean currents rub against each other. But scientists are fairly sure that once the fish reach freshwater, they use their sense of smell to reach home. Salmon can recognize their home stream years later, even if the river has changed.

After the yolk sacs are absorbed, the young salmon, called alevins, begin to catch their own food, mostly insects. Of an average brood of 7,500 alevins, only about 4 survive to migrate to the sea.

The salmon eggs lie buried in gravel in streambeds until they hatch. Gravel keeps the eggs from washing away. For the first few days after they are laid, the eggs are very fragile—a person walking in a streambed can destroy thousands of eggs.

Tiny salmon hatch in late winter and spring. They hide in gravel for a few weeks feeding off the contents of their yolk sacs until they are larger.

5

In estuaries, places where freshwater and saltwater meet, the smolts make the change to saltwater fish. They are now adult salmon.

4

In streams or lakes, finger-long salmon called parr leave their homes after just a few days or as long as 18 months (it depends on the species of salmon). When parr start to migrate to the sea, they are called smolts. Between 30 and 70 percent of the smolts may perish before they reach the river's mouth. At the river's mouth, another 5 to 35 percent may be eaten by birds or larger fish.

6

Pacific salmon live in the ocean from one to four years (depending on their species) before making their one and only trip back up the river to the place they were born. There they spawn and then die.

The young salmon hatch and hide under the gravel for several weeks. During that time they live off a built-in food supply, a yolk sac that hangs beneath them like a lunch bag.

As winter turns to spring, the tiny salmon begin to hatch. After a few weeks, they wriggle out of the gravel to feed on insects that drift downstream or fall into the water from overhanging trees.

On their way to the sea, salmon pass through tidal marshes and shallow bays called estuaries. It is in these places where saltwater and freshwater meet that salmon make an amazing transformation from freshwater fish to saltwater fish. They have to do this to leave the river and enter the sea. Pacific salmon stay in the ocean for up to four years before making their one and only trip back to their home stream to breed and die.

Since the early 1800s, when the Lewis and Clark expedition opened up the Northwest, wild salmon have been pushed by humans to near extinction. Settlers built dams across the rivers to create water power and to control flooding. The dams reduced the rivers' flow and blocked the way for migrating salmon.

As people took more water from the rivers for power stations, crops, and drinking water, even less water was left in the streams for the salmon. Logging and clearing land for farms removed shade trees that cooled the rivers and anchored the soil to the shore. Loosened soil washed into the streams, smothering salmon eggs and damaging the delicate gills of young fish. Streams and rivers next became the dumping grounds for the wastes of growing communities.

Many millions of salmon died, and those that survived cope with stresses that few other fishes have to face. Carl Schreck is a fish biologist with the Oregon Cooperative Fish and Wildlife Research Unit in Corvallis, Oregon. How does dealing with all these challenges, he wonders, affect a salmon's ability to avoid predators, find food, resist disease, mature, and reproduce?

The salmon has to be in peak condition for its trip, like a marathoner ready for competition. "The fish has to be in great physical shape if it is going to make the trip successfully. What we're trying to do is determine what good physical fitness for the salmon is, and what stress factors affect it." Carl and his team study food supply, overcrowding, and

There are many different species of salmon. These are Chinook salmon parr. Chinook salmon are very large salmon that live in northern Pacific waters. They can migrate to the ocean the first to second year of life and remain there for up to another three years or so.

Carl Schreck (left) and other researchers at work in a major river. They are listening for the signals of released salmon that have been tagged for tracking. The signals can tell them where the fish go and how far down they are swimming.

other stresses that affect the fish. They also trace the fish's resistance to disease. They are trying to find out how salmons' health and response to stress could change their growth and development.

Like a detective, Carl conducts investigations in the field and the laboratory. "First we try to understand the environment that fish have to operate in," he says. If there is a dam on the river they are studying, the biologists return to the lab and build something similar.

The biologists duplicate the stress of a dam in the laboratory and measure changes in fish as they try to overcome the problem. Carl explains, "Laboratory information can tell you what an animal *can* do. Field work tells you what an animal *does* do." From his work in the lab and in the field, he has found that when you impose a stress on a salmon, you can affect the salmon's development.

Carl has found that salmon respond to stresses, such as a dam (where little fish have big problems getting downstream and adult fish can't easily move upstream) or polluted water, by not growing up. When confronted by too much stress, some salmon don't mature and don't make the change from freshwater to saltwater fish.

Carl is now concentrating his investigation in estuaries. It's here that a salmon's change from a freshwater to a saltwater fish often takes place. Salmon may spend anywhere from hours to weeks in an estuary as they make their way from streams to the ocean. Carl and his team track the salmon by radio, aircraft, and boat so they can know the salmon's exact location at all times. They also record the saltiness of the water. So far, they have discovered that the fish travel well in the river. But when they enter the estuary, instead of moving into salty water, they are likely to stay in the less salty surface layer, where they are then eaten by hungry birds.

Researcher Carl Schreck studies animal physiology, which he describes as "sports medicine for fishes." Here Carl is drawing blood from a young salmon to measure the amount of stress-related hormones the blood contains.

Saving the Salmon

Salmon awareness is spreading. Students like these at Pigeon Creek in Washington state (below) are going to streams to study migrating salmon.

But students aren't just studying salmon. They are also getting involved. These students (right) are helping clean up the streams in which salmon travel.

How do we help stressed salmon? Scientists like Carl Schreck are working with citizens at all levels, from state leaders to school kids, to save the salmon. Carl's work helps planners understand what makes a good habitat for salmon. He also helps communities find ways to help salmon go around dams. One way is to build fish ladders, a series of steps like an underwater staircase that fish can use to move upstream. Another way is to drive fish around dams in water-filled trucks. Carl's research also helps improve ways to raise salmon in fish hatcheries, which can provide new fish to increase the population in the wild.

Organizations are also involved. Salmon Watch is an environmental education program that takes students to streams where Pacific salmon are spawning and dying. Watching salmon bravely struggle to reach their home stream leaves many students committed to aiding their journey. Adopt-a-Stream is another program that teaches young people how to preserve rivers and streams where young salmon live and develop. Students clean streams, add gravel to streambeds, or plant trees by banks. "What's really important is the protection of the water," says Carl. "If we make it good enough for salmon, it will also be good for people, for agriculture, and for other uses."

6

UNSOLVED MYSTERIES

When studying the mysteries of the sea, scientists often answer one question only to find two more.

"These are much deeper waters than I'd thought," mused Sherlock Holmes. His observation is particularly fitting for the study of the ocean. The surface of the moon has been mapped more thoroughly than the ocean floor. NASA astronauts have spent days on the moon. But the deepest part of the ocean, 10,800 meters (about 36,000 feet) down, has been visited once, for only half an hour. That may be part of the reason so many mysteries of the sea remain unsolved.

Researchers using scientific inquiry methods have solved some of the ocean's mysteries, but as soon as they answer one question, they uncover many more. And all the evidence that scientists have uncovered so far points to the fact that there is little time to waste in saving many different animals in the ocean. Many animals are nearing extinction levels, or levels at which their populations are so low that they may not be able to recover.

Humans are affecting the ocean in potentially devastating ways. Overfishing on Georges Bank, adding pollution to the fragile coral reefs, contributing to the warming of the Antarctic, and blocking salmon migration routes can either hurt marine animals or damage their environment.

(above)
Satellite images can show heat patterns around the globe. This satellite image shows land temperatures. The hottest places are yellow. The coolest places are dark blue. Images like this one help scientists measure global temperature changes.

(left)
Unraveling scientific mysteries often calls for long days at sea.

(right)
German Mendez, an environmentalist in Cozumel, Mexico, works to help coral reefs. He transplants live coral from dying habitats to thriving habitats where the coral can grow.

(below)
In recent years, people have tried adding to what the sea can provide through aquaculture. First practiced thousands of years ago by the Chinese and Japanese, aquaculture is agriculture in water. Here fish are being raised in cages suspended from floating platforms in the water off Hong Kong.

Some people are working to change the ways humans affect oceans and ocean life. To reduce overfishing, fishers, scientists, conservationists, and government officials must work together. These groups have traditionally been suspicious of each other, often having different ideas as to how best to manage fish stocks. The GLOBEC project brings these groups together to find a solution. For example, fishers gather data about the health of Georges Bank and share stories from years of working the fishing grounds with GLOBEC scientists.

Aquaculture may help restore fish and coral populations. Aquaculture is the science, business, and art of raising aquatic plants and animals. "Fish farmers" raise salmon, oysters, mussels, and other sea life in science labs and ocean inlets to help restock the oceans. Corals are being raised at the Pittsburgh Zoo for aquariums and medical research so that we don't need to remove coral from the reefs. Even elementary students are getting into the aquaculture business. Some schools are hatching salmon eggs and releasing young fish into local rivers.

But the news on aquaculture isn't all good. Research has found that fish farming in shallow waters can lead to pollution of the water by fish wastes. Also, the fish that are raised often eat many times their own weight in smaller fish, which can deplete an area's resources. Can we manage aquaculture in ways that preserve the environment? It's another question for scientists to answer.

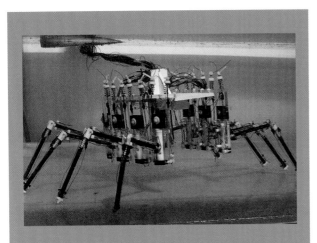

Robot Lobster

Imagine a platoon of metal lobsters patrolling the coasts of the United States, collecting data on water quality and pollution levels. Their designer, Joseph Ayers, a professor at Massachusetts' Northeastern University, studies how lobsters move, behave, and survive. He's using this information to design a metal robot lobster to monitor the health of the oceans.

Each robot lobster will likely cost about $300 to build, making it possible to create an affordable army of ocean inspectors. The information they provide may help solve more of the unsolved mysteries of the ocean.

Scientists also want to provide safe places for the fishes that are already living in the sea. WHOI biologist Rich Harbison has researched the history of the fishing industry and its current crisis. He would like to see marine preserves, places set aside for the protection of ocean animals, closed to all fishing.

"Who knows if the [population of cod is] down because of fishing pressure or because their habitat is being destroyed?" Rich wonders. "If parts of the ocean are put aside where there is no fishing at all, these may provide an opportunity to see what the environment is like if there is no dragging [fishing using bottom-dragging nets] for twenty or thirty years. Rather than putting a limit on the number of fishes that can be caught, say to fishers, 'We're setting aside some of the bottom so the fish can reproduce. Later you may catch even more fish than you're catching now.'"

Some areas in the ocean are already being protected. The National Oceanic and Atmospheric Administration located in Washington, D.C., oversees preserves in 12 ocean sites and 22 estuary sites. Since 1972 these areas have become laboratories and classrooms where the effects of human activities are studied. In these places what people want to do takes second place to what's important for the ocean.

Scientists like Rich Harbison would like to try doing experiments in marine preserves. The answers scientists find there may help answer the question of how to bring back disappearing fishes.

Most people don't realize that what they do in their own communities could have an impact on the ocean, even though it may be hundreds of miles away. Pollution that flows into streams and rivers is often hard to trace because it comes from many different sources, such as oil from parking lots, fertilizers from farms and golf courses, and sewage from some treatment plants. But much of the pollution ends up flowing downhill to the sea.

Those who work to save the salmon have shown that you don't have to be a scientist to help preserve ocean life. Cleaning up the water that flows into the sea is a critical first step, and supporting pollution reduction along the coasts helps keep the water clean. The things you do can have a global impact.

One of the biggest effects on the world's oceans, from the poles to the equator, is warming temperatures. From the Antarctic to the tropical reefs, a rise in ocean temperature is a serious threat to plants and animals. Some people believe our planet is in a normal warm cycle, but

Sometimes people have to step in to help after a natural disaster. Greg Locken of the Washington Department of Fisheries put wild coho salmon into the Toutle River in Washington state. The salmon runs in this part of the river were destroyed by silt, mud, and the destruction of shade trees, all a result of the eruption of Mt. St. Helens. Debris from the eruption can be seen on the riverbank.

A teacher and a student in a Fall River, Massachusetts, high school are raising quahogs, a kind of clam, to release later into the wild.

many agree that greenhouse gases could be contributing to the temperature changes. Whatever we can do to use less energy, from turning off lights to walking rather than driving, can help slow global warming. Even small things that you do can help reduce greenhouse gases and clean up the air and seas.

Most scientists agree that it is important to know much more about the environment we hope to preserve. To do that, we need to look at the ocean even more closely than is possible using ships, submersibles, or satellites.

Woods Hole oceanographers Scott Gallager and Peter Wiebe imagine what it would be like to work in what they think of as the ultimate ocean laboratory—an underwater observatory where several scientists could live and work for three to six months at a time. To Scott, this would be "a window into another world. It would also have equipment and instruments that allow us to make frequent observations so we can see changes as they happen to help create that big picture."

But scientists can't do all the work themselves. They need to join forces with trained amateurs. Tom Goreau hopes to establish an international network of scuba divers to help him track coral bleaching. Recreational divers would learn to recognize and report cases of coral bleaching. They would all be connected through the Internet.

Bird watchers living on several continents help keep track of migrating Antarctic birds. The data they provide help scientists like Susan and Wayne Trivelpiece better understand these changing populations.

Carl Schreck's work with salmon is supported by students and other volunteers. In an effort to clean up watersheds, people regularly test the water quality of their local rivers and streams. Their ongoing investigations have helped track down and eliminate pollution before it reaches the ocean.

Over the ages people have turned to the oceans for wealth, for inspiration, and to unlock its secrets. Oceanographers go to sea for some of the same reasons. What they learn will enrich not only our lives, but the life of the ocean as well.

Ocean detectives will continue to sail the ocean for many years to come, finding answers to new mysteries in the sea.

GLOSSARY

algae [AL-jee] Seaweed or one-celled aquatic plants.

aquaculture [AHK-wah-cul-chur] The science, business, and art of raising aquatic plants and animals.

bank Shallow underwater area made of sand and gravel.

calcium carbonate [CAL-see-um CAR-buh-nate] A compound found in limestone, marble, corals, crab shells, teeth, bones, and dissolved in seawater.

continental shelf A rim of shallow ocean floor that runs around the edges of continents. Continental shelves are part of continents. They make up less than 10 percent of the total area of the oceans, but most ocean life is found there.

copepod [KOH-peh-pod] A shrimp-like zooplankton that is a key animal in the ocean food web.

coral bleaching A natural disaster in which most or all of the corals' plant partners, the zooxanthellae, are absent.

echo sounder See sonar.

ecosystem How living and non-living things and their environment function as a unit.

estuary [ES-choo-air-ee] A place, often a protected bay at the mouth of a river, where freshwater and saltwater mix.

food web The connections between animals in an ecosystem, shown by which animal eats which plant or other animal; several interlinked food chains.

Georges Bank Part of the Atlantic continental shelf that extends seaward almost 321 kilometers (200 miles) east from the coast of Massachusetts, famous for its fishing.

global warming The theory that carbon dioxide and other gases produced by burning fossil fuels are trapped in the upper atmosphere, absorbing and reflecting heat back to Earth.

GLOBEC Short for Global Ocean Ecosystems Dynamics, the program was formed to study how climate change might affect life in the world's oceans.

hypothesis [hy-POTH-i-sis] An educated guess or question that further research will prove or disprove.

indicator species An animal or plant that is typical of an ecosystem. Looking at what is happening to an indicator species can provide clues about what is happening to the other animals and plants in that area.

invertebrate [in-VUR-teh-brit] An animal without a backbone. About 95 percent of the animals in the ocean are invertebrates.

krill Small, shrimplike creatures that exist in large numbers in Antarctic waters (and elsewhere). They are an important food for many other animals.

larval An adjective describing a newly hatched animal that looks very different from its adult stage.

limestone See calcium carbonate.

mass bleaching Coral bleaching that happens across large areas of ocean.

microzooplankton Microscopic animal plankton.

molt To shed skin.

NASA The National Aeronautics and Space Administration, a government agency that oversees space exploration and research.

nutrient A nourishing substance.

oceanographer A scientist who studies the physical, chemical, biological, or geological features of the ocean.

organism An individual animal or plant.

pack ice Floating ice that is formed from seawater at the beginning of winter, forming one big mass.

parr A young salmon.

physiology [fiz-ee-AHL-uh-jee] The study of how the body works.

phytoplankton [fy-toe-PLANK-ten] Microscopic plants suspended in water, base of the food chain in the sea.

plankton Tiny animals and plants that drift with the ocean currents. These include microscopic plants and animals as well as the larval stages of many sea creatures, such as fish, crabs, and lobsters.

polyp [PAHL-ip] The non-swimming stage of a coral. The animal looks like a hollow cup with tentacles surrounding the open end.

predator An animal that eats other animals.

prey An animal that is eaten by other animals.

scientific inquiry The logical process by which all scientists seek to solve the mysteries of the world.

smolt A salmon old enough to adapt to saltwater.

sonar A device for detecting objects underwater by reflection of sound waves; also called echo sounder.

spawn To lay eggs.

symbiotic relationship Two different species living together.

yolk sac A built-in food supply that some fish have when they are newly hatched. The yolk sac nourishes the baby fish for a few weeks.

zooplankton [zoh-PLANK-ten] Animal plankton.

zooxanthellae [zoh-uh-zan-THEL-ee] One-celled algae living in the tissues of reef-building corals.

FURTHER READING

Blashfield, Jean F. *Antarctica.* Austin, TX: Raintree Steck-Vaughn, 1995.

Cerullo, Mary. *Coral Reef: A City That Never Sleeps.* New York: Cobblehill, 1996.

Cone, Molly. *Come Back, Salmon.* San Francisco: Sierra Club Books, 1992.

Kovacs, Deborah, and Kate Madin. *Beneath Blue Waters: Meeting with Remarkable Deep-Sea Creatures.* New York: Viking, 1996.

Kress, Stephen, Pete Salmansohn, and the National Audubon Society. *Project Puffin: How We Brought Puffins Back to Egg Rock.* Gardiner, ME: Tilbury House, 1997.

Massa, Renato. *The Coral Reef.* Austin, TX: Raintree Steck-Vaughn, 1998.

McMillan, Bruce. *Penguins at Home: Gentoos of Antarctica.* Boston: Houghton Mifflin, 1993.

McMillan, Bruce. *Summer Ice: Life Along the Antarctic Peninsula.* Boston: Houghton Mifflin, 1995.

Poucet, S. *Antarctic Encounter: Destination South Georgia.* New York: Simon and Schuster, 1995.

Taylor, Barbara. *Look Closer: Coral Reef.* New York: Dorling Kindersley, 1992.

INDEX

Acknowledgments

The author wishes to acknowledge the help and support of the following people who were interviewed for this book: Cabell Davis, Scott Gallager, Thomas Goreau, Rich Harbison, Larry Madin, Dorinda Ostermann, Carl Schreck, Susan Trivelpiece, Wayne Trivelpiece, and Peter Wiebe. The author would also like to thank Audrey Bryant, Deborah Kovacs, and Kate Madin for their ongoing help and support.

Credits

The Sherlock Holmes quote on page 5 is from "The Blue Carbuncle," in *The Adventures of Sherlock Holmes* by Sir Arthur Conan Doyle, Oxford, England: Oxford University Press, 1993. The Sherlock Holmes quote on page 53 is from "The Reigate Squires," in *Memoirs of Sherlock Holmes* by Sir Arthur Conan Doyle, Oxford, England: Oxford University Press, 1993.

All photographs are courtesy of Woods Hole Oceanographic Institution (WHOI), except for the following:

Alevison, Bill: 28, 29; Animals, Animals: 39; Ayers, Joseph/Northeastern Marine Science Center: 56; Commonwealth of Massachusetts: 11; Hilbertz, Wolf: 31, Back Cover; Huss, Chris: 47, 55; Kleindinst, Tom/WHOI: 6,7,16; Larison, Jim: 5; Madin, Larry: 2 top three small pictures, 17, 20 far left; National Aeronautics and Space Administration (NASA): 4 top left; National Geographic Society: 21 bottom right inset, 42, 54, 57; Porter, James W.: 30; Preston, Louisa: 23, 26; Rotman, Jeff: Front Cover, 1, 2-3 bottom center, 21 top right, 22, 24, 27; Samuels, Amy/Chicago Zoological Society: 21 lower right; Schreck, Carl: 48, 49; SeaWIFS Project, NASA/Goddard Space Flight Center and ORBIMAGE: 52; Sission, Robert: 25; Society for the Preservation of New England Antiquities (SPNEA): 10; The Standard Times, New Bedford, MA: 58; Trivelpiece, Susan and Wayne: 3 right, 32, 35, 36, 37 top, 38, 40, 41; Wheelwright, Sidnee: 43, 46, 50, 51; Wiebe, Peter/WHOI: 4 right two small pictures

Art:

Illustrations on pages 4, 9 right sidebar, 14, and 21 middle center are by Elisabeth Broughton.

Illustrations on pages: 8–9 center, 15, 25 inset, and 44–45 are by Katherine Brown-Wing.

The illustration at the top of pages 20–21 is by Patricia Wynne.